Jim Arnosky

Look at Me!

WILD ANIMAL SHOW-OFFS

STERLING CHILDREN'S BOOKS
New York

FOR BILLY AND LAUREN

STERLING CHILDREN'S BOOKS
New York

An Imprint of Sterling Publishing Co., Inc.
1166 Avenue of the Americas
New York, NY 10036

ISBN 978-1-4549-2809-6

Distributed in Canada by Sterling Publishing Co., Inc.
c/o Canadian Manda Group, 664 Annette Street
Toronto, Ontario M6S 2C8, Canada

For information about custom editions, special sales, and premium and corporate purchases, please contact Sterling Special Sales at 800-805-5489 or specialsales@sterlingpublishing.com.

Manufactured in China

Lot #:
2 4 6 8 10 9 7 5 3 1
06/18

sterlingpublishing.com

Cover and interior design by Heather Kelly
The artwork in this book was created using pencil, white chalk, and acrylic paints.

CONTENTS

 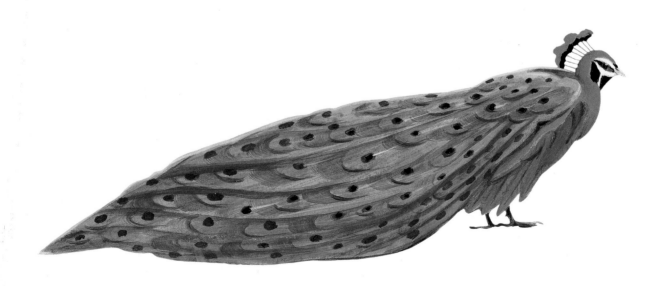

Each feather eye is made up of long, narrow feather barbules, each possessing a tiny portion of the overall color pattern created when combined with all the other feathers.

When not displaying, a peacock drags its huge, heavy tail behind it like a packed-up traveling show.

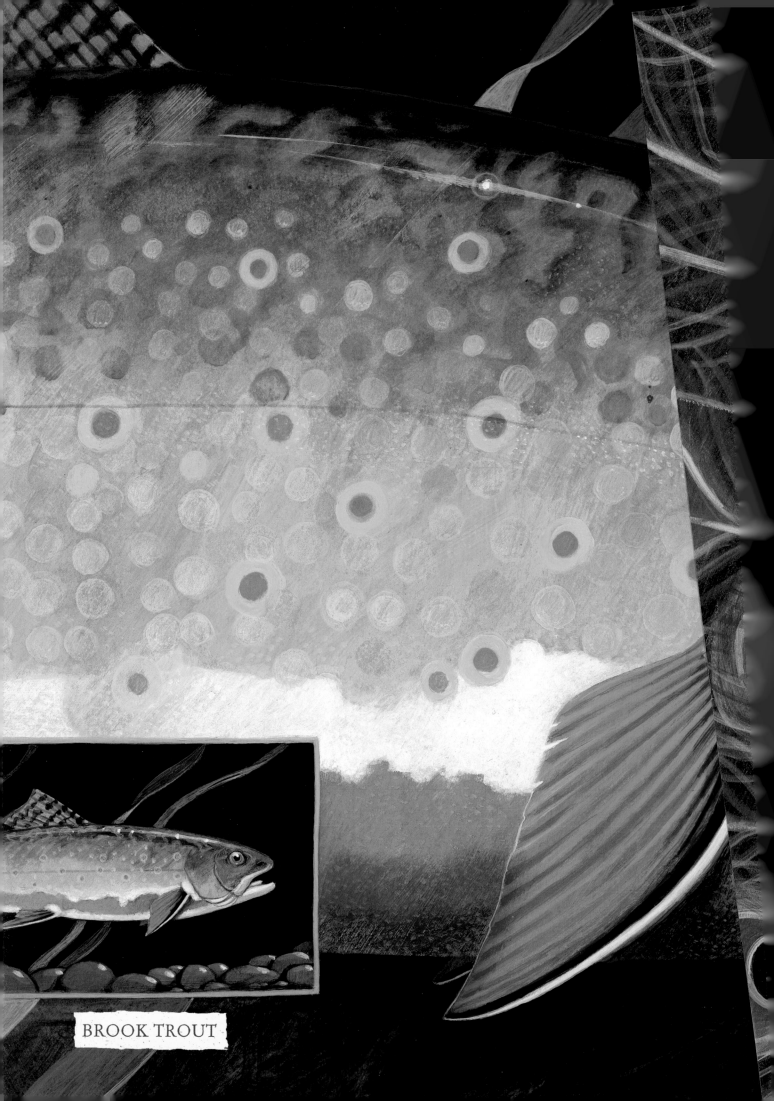

BROOK TROUT

Like the peacock, a male turkey will fan its tail
to display its dominance in the flock or enlarge
itself to confront a rival. And to add to the show,
a turkey fanning its prodigious tail will also strut
boldly and gobble loudly.

TURKEY WITH
TAIL FOLDED

Male turkeys have
beards on their chests made
up of long hairs. A long beard
signifies an older male and
superior mate.

Introduction

Whenever I view a distant bird up close through my camera's telephoto lens or hold a glistening trout in my hands as I release it back into the water, I am awestruck by their beauty. Why are wild animals so stunningly beautiful? What is the purpose of their showy displays and bold markings? One reason is that in the natural world the sounds of most animals are muted by the ambient noise of wind, water, and rustling leaves. A bold stripe or brilliant spot of color can be a kind of visible language enabling wildlife to communicate silently.

Every eye-catching color display or marking in animals is designed to attract or repel other animals. Some displays are immediately obvious. For instance, the male ruby-throated hummingbird's throat patch is black until it flashes ruby red in the sunlight. Some attraction displays are more subtle, such as the gradual brightening of overall color in the scales of certain fish. In many species, breeding season brings on color changes that greatly enhance an animal's physical appearance. During this time, when animals want to stand out rather than blend in, these colorful changes aid males in attracting mates. From a distance, humans can see only a hint of this brilliance. Imagine how impressive such finery appears up close, the way other animals see it!

Let's look at some of the ways animals show off as they display their finery and transform themselves in surprising ways to attract attention, confuse a predator, or frighten off a rival.

Jim Arnosky

The red flash of color on a ruby hummingbird's throat is created by the angle of reflected sunlight.

Spruce Grouse

At left, a male brook trout during spawning season seen up close the way another trout might see it. The small boxed image shows the whole trout.

During mating season, male grouse fan their tails to expose bold bars of color and strut around to establish territory and impress female grouse.

Ruffled Grouse

FRILLED LIZARD

FANNED TAILS

Behold the glorious peacock! When fully displayed,
a peacock's spectacular tail is four feet wide and two feet high.
That's eight square feet of tail! Combined with the bird's loud,
raucous call, a displaying peacock gets plenty of attention.
And that's exactly why they fan their tail feathers—to get the
attention of a mate or, in the case of the peacock's uniquely
designed tail feathers, to suddenly confront an approaching
enemy with an army of fierce-looking feather "eyes."

Skin Spreaders

Some lizards and snakes spread the loose skin around their heads and necks to express alarm or show aggression. To make itself appear larger and more ferocious, the frilled lizard of Australia raises and spreads its neck skin to form an umbrella-like collar. This impressive frill of skin combined with a gaping mouth warns, "BACK OFF! I'm big and I bite!" But the threat is a hollow one. If the display doesn't frighten away a would-be attacker, the frilled lizard takes off running as fast as it can.

Anoles fan out their throats to attract mates. In the Everglades, I have patiently watched many of these small lizards, waiting for them to spread and display their bright orange throat fans. Seeing the colorful fan suddenly appear is one of my favorite wildlife moments.

A snake's body is all ribcage from the neck to the tail. A cobra's ominous-looking hood is created when the snake raises its head and spreads the slender rib bones in the neck, pulling the skin taut. Cobras aren't the only snakes that do this; the deadly mamba and the harmless hognose snake also "hood up" when threatened.

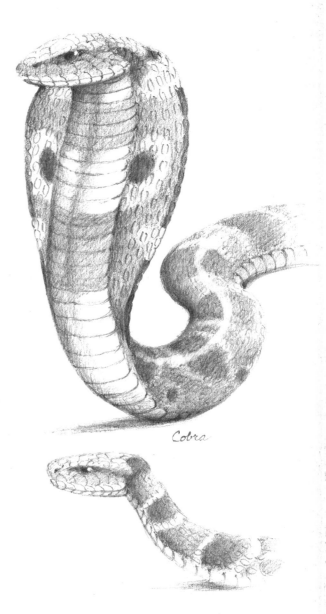

Cobra

Without its hood display, a cobra looks similar to other snakes.

Anole with and without throat fan spread

When not spread, the frilled lizard's frill hangs down like a closed umbrella, as you see at lower left.

DIAMONDBACK RATTLESNAKE

Noise Makers

Rattlesnakes are well camouflaged for protection against predators and for stealth when stalking prey. They blend so well with their surroundings that you can actually walk right by or, in rocky areas, step right over a rattler and never know it. To avoid being accidentally trampled by large, heavy animals (including humans), a rattlesnake vibrates the hard, hornlike rattles at the end of its tail. The loud buzzing sound warns anyone nearby of the snake's presence.

The rattlesnake's rattle begins as a single hard stub at birth, and each year a new rattle segment grows, loosely connected to the last. The sound of a rattlesnake rattling will stop an approaching animal in its tracks.

Other animals also use sound to get attention. The male ruffed grouse hops on a hollow log and beats its wings against the air, creating a far-reaching drumming sound to attract a mate. A beaver will suddenly slap its big flat tail on the water surface to say emphatically, "GO AWAY! THIS PLACE IS MINE!" A bullfrog inflates its throat, gathering air to release into a loud, deep-throated mating call. And during mating season, a big bull alligator can bellow for the company of a mate so loudly that it sounds more like a roar. When an alligator does this, its body vibrates so strongly that the water pooled on its back rains upward into the air in a shower of tiny droplets.

Ruffed grouse on "drumming" log

Beaver tail slap

Bullfrog calling

Bellowing alligator with water vibrating up off its back

MAGNIFICENT FRIGATEBIRDS

Inflators

Certain species of animals inflate themselves to appear bigger and more formidable to enemies. Some types of birds do this to show off during breeding season. To attract a mate, the male magnificent frigatebird perches at the top of a suitable nest site and inflates its highly elastic, crimson-colored throat skin. This bizarre display in which the bird's head is almost entirely hidden behind the throat balloon is something female frigatebirds find very attractive. Soon a pair of frigatebirds are building their nest.

Inflation isn't only used to attract or impress a mate. Both male and female puffer fish puff themselves up whenever they are threatened by predators. The African bullfrog can inflate its body to twice its normal size to avoid being swallowed whole by a frog-eating snake.

During breeding season, a male prairie chicken inflates its orange throat skin in two places, one on each side of its neck.

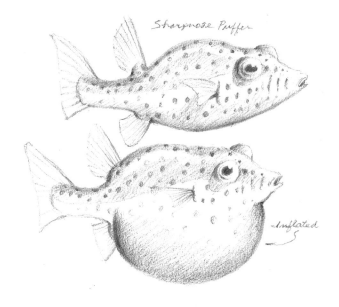

During daylight hours, frigatebirds rarely come ashore. Their amazing soaring ability keeps them out over the ocean, where they watch the surface for fish to eat. In the evening they all come in to roost on shoreline trees and electrical wires.

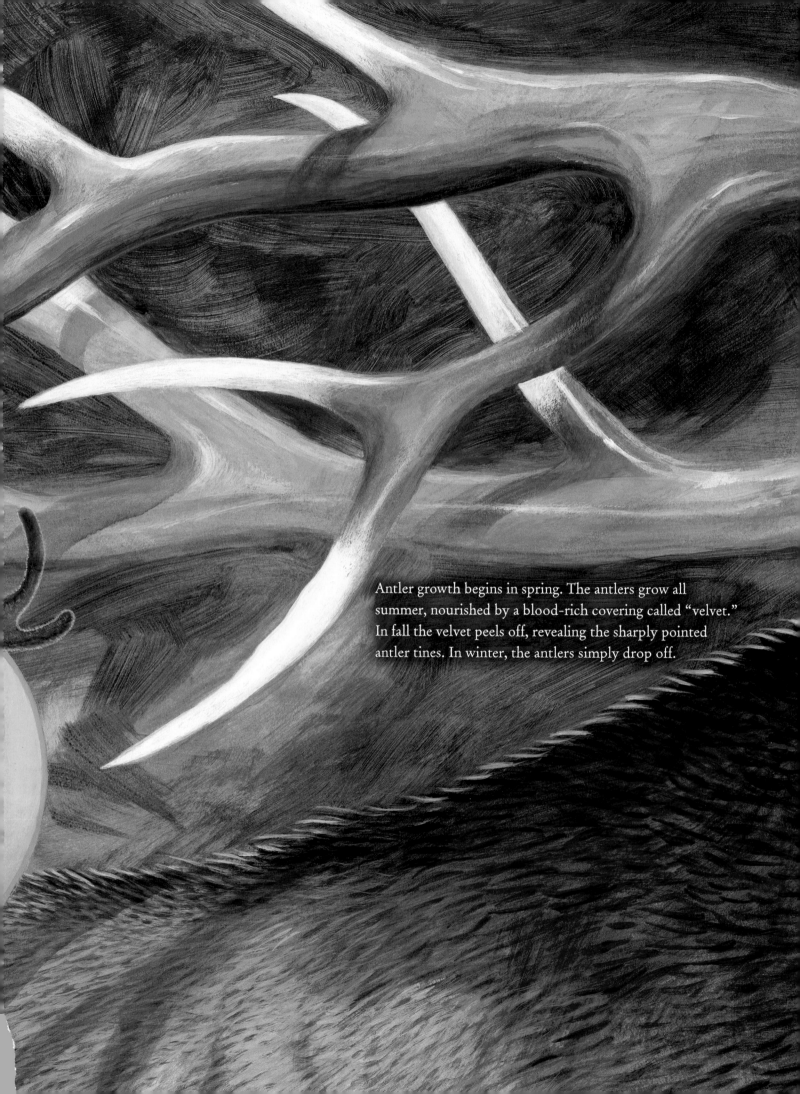

Antler growth begins in spring. The antlers grow all summer, nourished by a blood-rich covering called "velvet." In fall the velvet peels off, revealing the sharply pointed antler tines. In winter, the antlers simply drop off.

MORE ABOUT ANTLERS

They may be temporary, but while they
adorn the head of a deer, moose,
or elk, antlers stand out as a
magnificent display of physical health,
strength, and power. And the vision of
an antlered animal
in the wild, with
nothing but frosty air
between you and those
sharp points, is unforgettable.

ANTLERS IN
VELVET

BIGHORN SHEEP

16

In Wyoming I watched a herd of elk making their w
along a winding riverbank. The animals' hooves kicked
up dust that hung in the air like mist over their heads.
Here and there a big bull's antlers stood out in bold silhouet
slowly rising and dipping as the bull moved. It was an overwhelmin
wonderful thing to witness.

In addition to their standout headwear, bull elk and moose make a
mating call that sounds like a bugle. Besides attracting female elk (cows)
the bugling also attracts other bulls as a sort of challenge, in which case
the antlers are used as the weapon they are meant to be.

Horns and Antlers

Horns and antlers are both displays of power and dominance that male deer, goats, and sheep wear like crowns in their wild kingdoms. Just the sight of horns or antlers larger than its own can intimidate a potential rival.

Nature endows animals with horns and antlers solely for battle—not with predators, but with members of their own species. Males use their antlers or horns to fight for breeding rights, territory, and sometimes just for the sake of battle. Male deer will spar with slender trees just to keep in shape for real bouts with other deer. Young rams will bang heads and horns together in play. But every playful headbutt is a portent of the serious headbutting they will do when they grow up.

Horns are permanent and grow larger with age. Antlers are temporary. They grow and are shed each year, with every new annual growth larger than the last. Antlers are made of a solid bone-like material that is one of the strongest and fastest-growing substances in nature.

During the twelve- to fourteen-year lifespan of a bighorn sheep, its horns can grow from this . . .

. . . to this!

A full-grown bighorn ram acts as though he is king of the mountain. And in the bighorn's world, he is.

CORE OF HONEYCOMBED BONE

Outer horn

Bone

SHINY SHEATH OF HARDENED HAIR

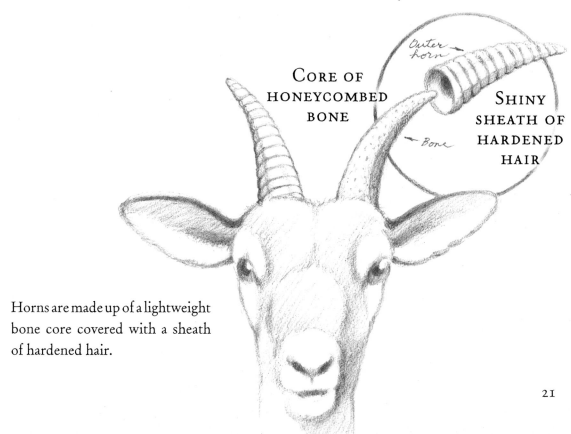

Horns are made up of a lightweight bone core covered with a sheath of hardened hair.

SOCKEYE SALMON

Color to Attract, Distract, or Warn

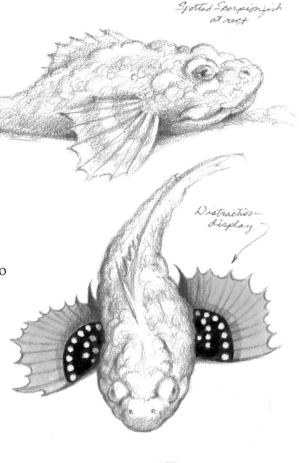

Spotted Scorpionfish at rest

In most species of fish, the males and females are similar in color. During spawning (breeding) season, the males become much more brilliant, but their overall colors and markings are the same as always. Sockeye salmon are a rarity in that spawning male and female sockeyes change their color completely from their overall blue-black to a bright red body and vivid green head. Spawning males undergo an added change. Their jaws elongate and become grotesquely hooked, giving them the appearance of ferocity. Why such an extreme change of color and facial features? To compete. To somehow stand out and show off among thousands of others swimming side by side, crowding their way upstream to their spawning grounds.

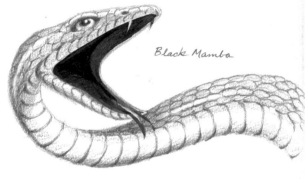

Distraction display

In the ocean, the spotted scorpionfish is nearly invisible as it blends with the muted and mottled colors of sand and coral. But when it is discovered by a predator, the scorpionfish flashes the hidden brilliance of color on the backs of its pectoral fins, which are usually held against the fish's body. The quick flash of color can distract an attacker just long enough for the scorpionfish to dash away, pectoral fins once again pressed against its sides, showing only the camouflaged brown-and-tan mottling that makes the fish so hard to see.

Black Mamba

Africa's black mamba snake is actually gray. Its name comes from the pitch-black color inside its mouth. When threatened, the snake opens its mouth wide to show the black inside. This is a warning: "Come no closer! I'm a black mamba and my venom is deadly!"

Poison frogs

Every species of poison frog in the South American rainforest is boldly marked and brightly colored to warn predators, "If you eat me, you will be very sick!"

23

WOOD DUCKS

The great egret (also called the common egret) was *not* very common one hundred years ago. Plume hunters supplying the decorative feathers for hats relentlessly drove the species to the verge of extinction. Once the shooting was outlawed, the egrets made a comeback. Today, the egret is common once again.

Bird Plumage

Whenever I see a bird momentarily fluff its feathers, then preen them back into place, I am reminded of the hidden beauty being tucked in—so many lovely feathers that could at any moment be fanned and displayed! Every bird possesses the ability to dazzle. Using binoculars, follow a bird with its wings outstretched, sailing downward to the earth. Watch closely how it folds those broad, long wings neatly under the feathers of its back. See how compact and contained wings can be.

The breeding plumage of birds is feathered beauty that simply cannot be contained. Even with wings folded, the standout beauty—and in some species, the special growth of breeding plumes—shows. These fancy plumes drag behind as the bird walks, or they can be raised high in the feather crests on certain birds' heads.

Ducks are among the most beautiful birds year-round, but during breeding season they become exquisite, with bolder colors and markings. What makes them so especially beautiful is the pleasing blending of color from feather to feather, creating the flawless markings that identify each species.

In some species of birds, the crest is spectacular. The hooded merganser's hatchet-shaped hood is actually a raised crest. When relaxed, the crest looks like long wet hair.

Hooded Merganser
[Male]

Crest down

Hooded Merganser
[Female]

The crests of birds can be very impressive displays. A bird will raise the feathers on its head to form a crest whenever it is agitated, alarmed, excited, or showing off.

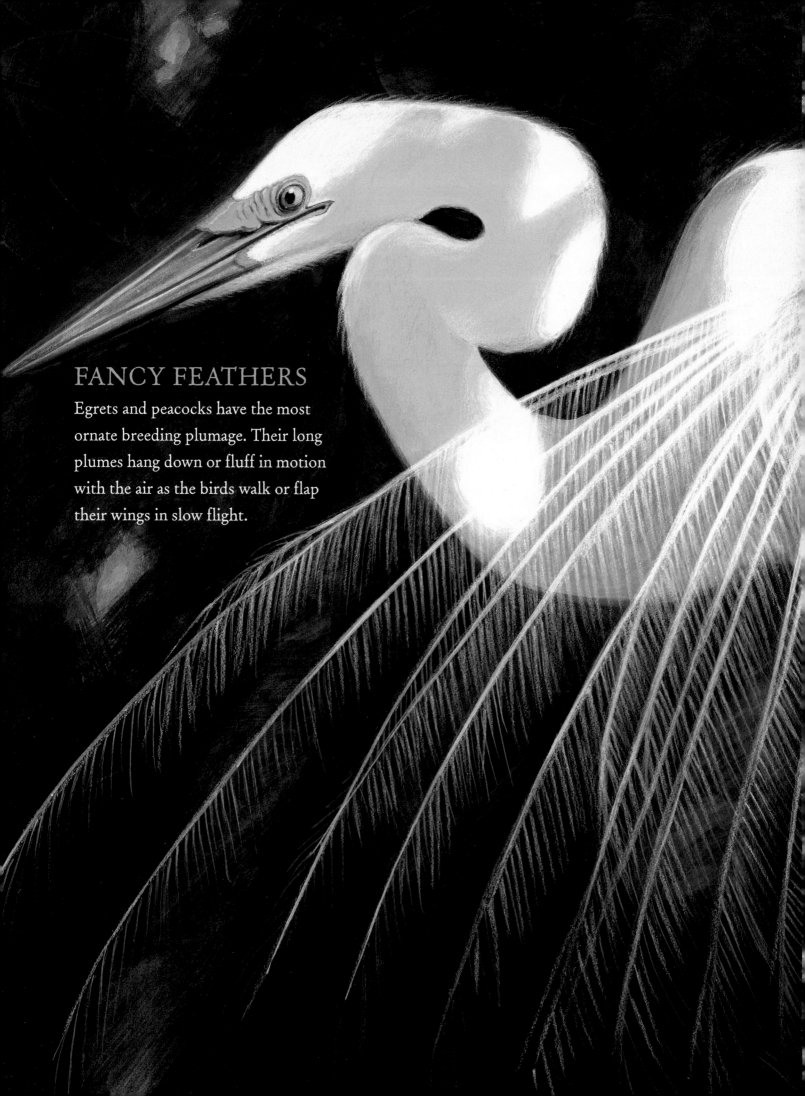

FANCY FEATHERS

Egrets and peacocks have the most
ornate breeding plumage. Their long
plumes hang down or fluff in motion
with the air as the birds walk or flap
their wings in slow flight.

Feathered Show-Offs

Of the many ways animals show off in order to stand out from the crowd, it is the spectacular breeding plumage of birds that outshines them all. To begin with, feathers are among the loveliest things in nature; almost as light as air, yet strong and resilient enough to withstand wind, rain, and snow. Birds completely encased in ice after a night of freezing rain thaw in the sun and fly again. Think of it! Feathers to keep birds warm and dry; feathers that create birds' colors and markings; feathers to line and cushion their nests; feathers to fly; feathers to blend into surroundings; feathers to create dazzling displays of beauty. In the animal kingdom, when it comes to showing off, I think the showiest show-offs are the birds, because of their fabulous feathers. What do you think?

Author's Note

A book is like a brook that flows from its source (the author) to distant places (readers everywhere). And as with a brook, you can trace a book back to its source—allowing you to discover what inspired and informed its creator. Looking now at the completed paintings and drawings in *Look at Me!*, I am reminded of the specific moments I experienced in nature that I was able to capture on paper.

For example, I once watched a spectacularly large and beautiful rattlesnake swim across a wilderness pool, pushing a path through lily pads to a place on the opposite bank, where it hid under some evergreen boughs. You can see this snake for yourself on page 12. How about the gorgeous ducks on page 24? Early one morning, I sat inside a cold and damp photography blind near our house, waiting for ducks to fly in. Just as I was about to give up, a spectacularly colored wood duck drake showed up right in the center of my camera lens! And the peacock you see on the cover of this book was one that confronted me boldly at the entrance of Spanish explorer Ponce de León's fabled Fountain of Youth Archaeological Park. A whole flock of peacocks patrol this famous and historic landmark, and after seeing the birds up close, I couldn't wait to get back to my studio to paint them.

While writing this book I learned many new things, from how exactly a cobra spreads its hood to what size hollow log a grouse typically chooses to perch on while drumming its wings against the air. As I wrote, I made decisions about which subjects I would illustrate in color and which I would draw in pencil. Everything in the art depended on what I was saying in the text, and while I worked on the art, I wrote and revised every sentence to bond art and text more closely together.

I began this book in springtime, surrounded by palm trees and the turquoise water of the Florida Keys. I finished it in the fall, within the quiet embrace of the Vermont farmhouse where I've completed most of my books. I hope it inspires you to spend time outdoors, watching for animal show-offs in your own area. There are animals everywhere saying, "Look at me!"

More About Animal Show-Offs

Arnosky, Jim. *Slither and Crawl.* New York, NY: Sterling Children's Books, 2015.

Arnosky, Jim. *Hidden Wildlife.* New York, NY: Sterling Children's Books, 2017.

Burnie, David. *DK Eyewitness Books: Bird.* New York, NY: DK Publishing, Inc., 2008.

Hawkins, Emily and Rachel Williams. *Atlas of Animal Adventures: A Collection of Nature's Most Unmissable Events, Epic Migrations and Extraordinary Behaviours.* New York, NY: Quarto, 2016.

Hickman, Pamela. *Animals and Their Mates: How Animals Attract, Fight for and Protect Each Other.* Toronto, ON: Kids Can Press, 2004.

Johnson, Rebecca L. *When Lunch Fights Back: Wickedly Clever Animal Defenses.* Minneapolis, MN: Lerner Publishing Group, 2014.

Kaner, Etta. *Animal Defenses: How Animals Protect Themselves.* Toronto, ON: Kids Can Press, 1999.

Parker, Steve. *DK Eyewitness Books: Fish.* New York, NY: DK Publishing, Inc., 2005.

Rake, Jody S. *Spines, Horns, and Armor: Animal Weapons and Defenses.* North Mankato, MN: Capstone Press, 2012.

Stewart, Melissa. *Feathers: Not Just for Flying.* Boston, MA: Charlesbridge, 2014.

Whitfield, Phil. *Weird and Wonderful: Attack and Defense: Astonishing Animals, Bizarre Behavior.* New York, NY: Macmillan, 2011.

Wilsdon, Christina. *Ultimate Reptileopedia: The Most Complete Reptile Reference Ever.* New York, NY: National Geographic Children's Books, 2015.

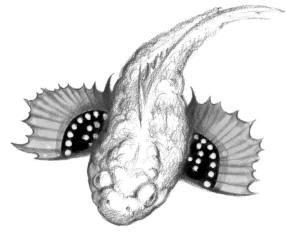

Other Books in this Series

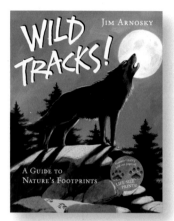

WILD TRACKS!
A Guide to Nature's Footprints

SLITHER AND CRAWL
Eye to Eye with Reptiles

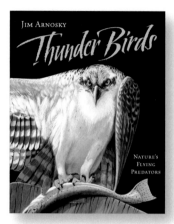

THUNDER BIRDS
Nature's Flying Predators

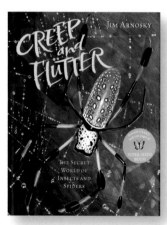

CREEP AND FLUTTER
The Secret World of Insects and Spiders

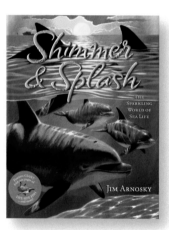

SHIMMER & SPLASH
The Sparkling World of Sea Life

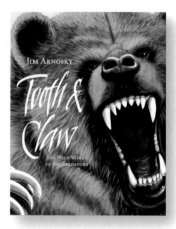

TOOTH & CLAW
The Wild World of Big Predators

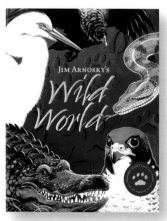

JIM ARNOSKY'S WILD WORLD

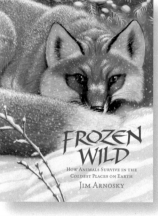

FROZEN WILD
How Animals Survive in the Coldest Places on Earth

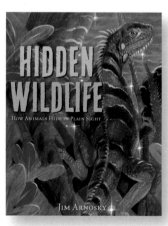

HIDDEN WILDLIFE
How Animals Hide in Plain Sight